MUMMIES

JOHN VORNHOLT has been an actor and a writer in children's theater and has written extensively for children's animated television shows. He is the author of *Masks*, a "Star Trek: The Next Generation" novel as well as a freelance journalist with credits in many magazines. He lives in Los Angeles, California.

MUMMIES

JOHN VORNHOLT

AN AVON  CAMELOT BOOK

For Will and Rick
Who know mummies never die;
Special thanks to Steven McDonald, Jean Durante, and Dennis and Mel Livesey

MUMMIES is an original publication of Avon Books. This work has never before appeared in book form.

AVON BOOKS
A division of
The Hearst Corporation
1350 Avenue of the Americas
New York, New York 10019

Copyright © 1991 by John Vornholt
Published by arrangement with the author
Library of Congress Catalog Card Number: 91-356
ISBN: 0-380-76317-6
RL: 6.6

Library of Congress Cataloging in Publication Data:
Vornholt, John.
    Mummies/John Vornholt.
        p.   cm.
    Summary: Examines mummies around the world and describes how they were created.
    1. Mummies—Juvenile literature. [1. Mummies.] I. Title.
    GT3340.V67   1991   91-356
    393'.3—dc20   CIP   AC

First Avon Camelot Printing: September 1991

CAMELOT TRADEMARK REG. U.S. PAT. OFF. AND IN OTHER COUNTRIES MARCA REGISTRADA, HECHO EN U.S.A.

Printed in the U.S.A.

OPM   10   9   8   7   6   5   4   3   2   1

Contents

Chapter 1

Why Mummies?

Imagine you're an archaeologist walking down a long, dark hallway. A flickering torch is your only light, and the air is choked with the dust of centuries. If you move your torch toward the wall, you see strange paintings of gods with human bodies and the heads of animals and birds.

Now you have to get down on your hands and knees and crawl through a tiny opening. Look out for trapdoors! They might plunge you down a shaft that is hundreds of feet deep. You've spent months exploring false passages, and you hope this isn't another one. Finally, you get through the opening and enter an eerie room that is full of silent figures.

These brittle mummies lie not in coffins but are piled against the wall like firewood. They are the servants, friends, and family of an Egyptian king, called a Pharaoh.

Some of the mummies in the room are not human—

they are cats, birds, crocodiles, and baboons. These people and pets are only a few of the things the Pharaoh will need in the afterlife. His spirits will come to stay with his mummified body in his tomb, so all his favorite things are here, including food and drink.

The Pharaoh's burial chamber is still far away, down another long corridor. Breathing is hard with the dust and the excitement, but you are walking faster. Are you the first person to see this tomb in thousands of years? Or have explorers and robbers been here many times over the centuries? They wouldn't bother the mummies

The entry chamber of King Tut's tomb, discovered by Lord Carnarvon and Howard Carter in 1922, shows evidence of having been ransacked by thieves. Fortunately only a few objects had been removed from the chamber. (The Metropolitan Museum of Art)

in the outer chamber, but will any of the king's gold remain?

After squeezing through a narrow crevice past a huge stone, you reach the inner burial chamber. This is a large room with a ceiling so high the light from your torch will not reach the top. Immense pillars surround the giant coffin, called a sarcophagus. As you feared, the gold is gone, and the boxes of treasure have been smashed open.

There is something else—a skeleton lying in a doorway where a rock fell on it. He was probably a grave robber who got careless—2000 years ago.

The sarcophagus is shaped like a loaf of bread and decorated with beautiful carvings. It stands nearly as tall as you and was chiseled from solid stone. You wonder how they ever got it in here. Excitedly, you call the others to help you open it, and you find another coffin inside. Like the toy that is one egg within another, you open coffin after coffin until reaching the last.

The last coffin contains the mummy of the Pharaoh. When you open it, you see a spectacular mask gilded in gold. The pleasant face on the mask smiles up at you, and you realize you are the first person to see the face of the king for over 3000 years.

Thick linen bandages wind around the mummy in a beautiful pattern. Underneath the wrappings are priceless amulets, pendants, and jewels which were put there to protect the king on his trip to the underworld. If you were a grave robber, you might plunge your hand into his chest and rip out the jewels. If you were an early explorer, you might take the mummy back to your hotel and unwrap it in front of applauding tourists. Thousands of mummies were destroyed in these ways.

You, however, are a modern archaeologist. You will save the precious mummy to be X-rayed and studied at a hospital or a university. From his blood type, you may discover which other mummies were his relatives. You'll find out how old he was, what health problems he had, and what killed him.

If you were to unwrap the mummy of the Pharaoh, you would find a body that smells of perfume instead of decay. His skin is hard and clings to fragile bone, but his hawk-nosed face still looks proud and peaceful. The Pharaoh is happy. His body has lasted thousands of years, and his name is spoken again. He is immortal.

Mummies Never Die

Except for the riches of King Tutankhamen, better known as King Tut, grave robbers took most of the treasure from Egyptian tombs a long time ago.

Today, scientists treat them with all the care and attention of precious artwork. Instead of removing their protective bandages, as researchers once did, they X-ray mummies to learn more about them. Autopsies and tests are performed on microscopic samples of their tissue, and the results tell us how these people lived—even what their dental care was like!

The Egyptians removed certain organs, such as the liver, brains, and intestines, and preserved them separately. Scientists perform genetic experiments on these tissue samples to find out how we have evolved from our ancient ancestors. We can learn where certain diseases came from and how they have changed over the centuries.

Archaeologists try to identify mummies by name and rank to tell us about governments and rulers of the past.

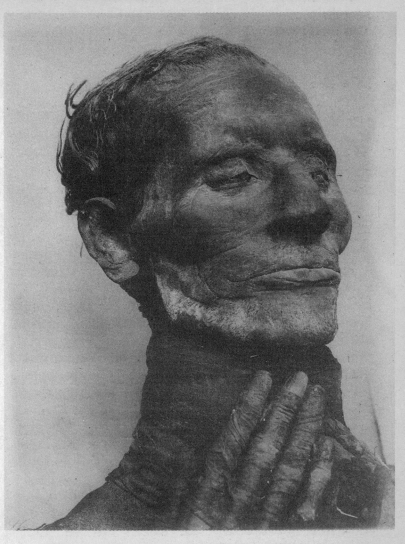

This mummy of an ancient Egyptian minister, discovered in 1905, is one of the best preserved mummies. (The Metropolitan Museum of Art)

Tomb paintings show us everyday life, historical events, and religious beliefs. Everything about a mummy tells us something.

Not All Mummies Are Egyptian

"Mummy" doesn't refer only to dead bodies from ancient Egypt. A mummy is any animal body that has been preserved in lifelike condition—with skin, bones, and hair intact.

Some mummies were created accidentally by heat, cold, or chemicals in the soil, but many ancient cultures—not just the Egyptians—intentionally preserved their dead for eternity. These include the Incas of Peru, Guanches of the Canary Islands, Scythians of Russia, Capuchins of Sicily, and early Chinese and Persian civilizations.

In fact, the word "mummy" comes from the Arabic word *moumia,* meaning bitumen. Bitumen is a chemical first used for embalming by the Byzantine Greeks! The Egyptians used a chemical called natron to dry out the body; then they treated it with resins and perfumes. They seldom used bitumen, but the word "mummy" stuck.

Although separated from Egypt by thousands of miles, other mummy-makers used many of the same techniques, but we'll never know as much about them as we know about Egyptian mummies. The Egyptians practiced this strange art for almost 3000 years, and they left beautiful tombs, paintings, and books to explain their practice.

One thing we do know: It was common for ancient people around the world to believe that the soul could not rest unless the body was kept lifelike.

Other Reasons for Mummies

Not all bodies were mummified to ensure immortality. Throughout history—even to the present day—the bodies of famous people have been preserved to honor them and inspire the living. These once-living statues are displayed like valuable artwork in air-tight, temperature-controlled cases.

That is how you can view the preserved body of the Russian revolutionary Vladimir Lenin in his tomb in Red Square, in Moscow. Russian embalmers have worked hard to keep Lenin's body in good condition, but the rumors are that his face is now mostly wax.

If you go to the Vatican in Rome, you can see the bodies of dozens of popes still lying in state. Some of them are less well-preserved than others. In some of the air-tight cases, you'll see skulls instead of faces. The embalmers of the Middle Ages were not nearly as skilled as the old Egyptians.

With the sad destruction of so many mummies over the centuries, we are lucky that numerous accidental mummies have been discovered. These are the bodies of ancient people who either fell or were thrown into peat bogs, caves, mines, and other places that naturally preserved their bodies for us to study today.

Despite what you have seen in old horror movies, the ancients did not believe that mummies were going to get up and walk again. They only wanted to preserve the body to keep the soul happy. So it may surprise you to learn that—in our own time—dead bodies are being preserved to be brought back to life in the future.

In a controversial process called cryonics, people can have their bodies quick-frozen immediately after death. These people believe their frozen bodies will be revived later, when there are cures for the diseases that killed them. This is a very expensive procedure, especially since the body must be stored indefinitely in a special freezer. However, it could provide a new source of mummies for future generations to study.

We value mummies today as much as the people who made them centuries ago, but for different reasons. They wanted to make a home for the soul, to honor the dead, and to find immortality. To us, mummies are unique visitors from the past who tell us how our ancestors lived—and died.

Chapter 2

Ancient Egypt—
Where Mummies Are
Immortal

The Nile River flows down the center of Egypt, and the land on both sides of it is wet and fertile. The rest of Egypt is a hot, dry desert with jagged mountains. Since recorded history, the Egyptians have used the fertile land around the Nile for growing food and housing the living. The desert was the only place left to bury the dead.

The Egyptians didn't like to burn their dead, because they thought fire was a living creature. To them, a body that was burning was being eaten by fire. They also didn't want the body to be eaten by animals or worms, so they were glad to bury their dead in the rocky desert where there was less chance of being eaten.

Long before the Egyptians made any mummies or built any tombs, they put bodies into pits and caves. They left a few simple pots, beads, and bits of food with the body for its trip to the underworld. Many of these bodies dried out before they could decay, and they became natural mummies, also called Coptic mummies.

Heat and dryness weren't the only necessary conditions for the preserved bodies. It also helped that the soil in the Egyptian desert was full of a natural salt, called natron. The discovery of natron was the first step toward full-scale mummification.

How Old Are Mummies?

In order to understand how old mummies are, you must understand the difference between years referred to as B.C. and A.D. B.C. means "Before Christ," and A.D. means "Anno Domini" (in the year of the Lord), and refers to the years since the birth of Christ. One of the most confusing things about this system is that B.C. years are counted backward from the birth of Christ. A.D. years, on the other hand, are counted forward from the birth of Christ. For example, 3000 B.C. is 3000 years before the birth of Christ, and 2000 B.C. is 2000 years before the birth of Christ.

We usually don't put the A.D. on a year—we simply say 1992, for example. However, if we say 1992 B.C., you should know it's almost 4000 years ago.

The first Egyptian attempts to mummify the dead took place around 3000 B.C., during a period called the Old Kingdom. They weren't very good at it then, and the mummies from that period are in poor condition. After centuries of practice, the Egyptians refined their techniques into an art form. They also developed complicated religious beliefs to explain why bodies *should* be mummified.

By 1500 B.C., in a period called the New Kingdom, everyone who could afford it had his body mummified. At one time, there must have been millions of mummies in tombs all along the Nile. To get some idea of how many, read these words from the Italian explorer Giovanni Belzoni, quoted by Mildred Mastin Pace in *Wrapped for Eternity,* talking about a tomb he searched in the early 1800s:

"It was so choked with mummies," he wrote, "I could not pass without putting my face in contact with some decayed Egyptians. But my own weight helped me on. However, I could not avoid being covered with bones, legs, and arms and heads rolling from above."

Another time, Belzoni wrote, "I sought a resting place, found one and contrived to sit. But when my weight bore on the body of an Egyptian, it crushed like a band-box. I sunk altogether among the broken mummies, with a crash of bones, rags, and wooden cases, which raised such a dust as kept me motionless for a quarter of an hour. I could not remove from the place, however, without increasing it and every step I took I crushed a mummy . . ."

Cities of the Dead

The first Egyptian tombs were like large flat buildings, and they were often built on streets lined with palm trees. It was not uncommon for the dead to have better houses than the living. During the Old Kingdom, mummification was reserved for royalty and important people in the Pharaoh's court. At that time, they

11

thought only the royalty could join the gods in the underworld.

As Egypt became a rich, powerful nation around 2700 B.C., the Pharaohs built bigger and bigger tombs for themselves. Around each royal tomb sprang little cities of smaller tombs, where lesser members of the Pharaoh's family and court were buried. A city of tombs for the dead is called a *necropolis.*

Around 2500 B.C., the Egyptians started building pyramids. Some Egyptian records suggest that the pyramid shape was discovered accidentally when workers made a mistake while building a box-like tomb called a *mastaba.* However it happened, pyramids became very popular, and at least 70 were built along the Nile.

Curiously, modern research has shown that certain shapes generate energy, and the pyramid is one of those shapes. Energy makes atomic particles move faster, lengthening their life. Even small pyramid models have been known to preserve food, discourage mold, and sharpen razor blades. Maybe the Egyptians knew that a pyramid would help preserve the Pharaoh's body.

In the city of Giza stand the great pyramids of Cheops, Chephren, and Mycerinus. Even-weathered by the ages, they are as awesome today as when they were built 4500 years ago.

Robbers of the Tomb

To satisfy religious beliefs and show how important they were, the Pharaohs went to the underworld with great riches. They were buried inside gold-plated coffins, surrounded by golden statues, jeweled amulets, and other amazing treasures. These ancient kings were all-powerful while they were alive, but dead, they feared grave robbers and went to great lengths to foil them. The first step was to hide the entrance which led inside the pyramid to the burial chamber. They often built fake entrances near the ground, while the real entrance was hidden underground or several levels up.

A confusing network of passages sloped downward to the burial chamber. This duplicated the path to the underworld and, it was hoped, confused the robbers.

Precautions didn't end there. Some pyramids had fake passageways, which led either nowhere or to deep pits, often hidden by trapdoors. The real passageways were often flooded with sand or blocked by stones weighing up to 45 tons. Curses were written on tablets and statues to scare away robbers, and the slaves who built the tombs were killed to keep them quiet.

Incredibly, none of those precautions worked. Every Egyptian pyramid and almost every tomb was plundered by grave robbers. Some were robbed only a few months after being built and sealed. This led to the theory that some robberies were "inside jobs" masterminded by the priests and architects who built these giant tombs.

The Golden Age of Mummies

We usually think of pyramids and mummies as going together, but mummification was still crude at the time of the great pyramids. It took another thousand years for the Egyptians to really get it right.

During the Middle Kingdom, which began about 2150 B.C., the Pharaohs lost some of their power. Kings in the north and south battled to control the country, and the capital moved around from Memphis to Thebes and other places. Priests became more numerous and more important, and religious beliefs became more complicated.

This was a good time for the mummy business, because priests convinced the common people that they could be immortal, too. Every Egyptian began to believe his soul could live as long as his body was preserved, and with more demand, the art of mummification blossomed.

By the time the New Kingdom began around 1550 B.C., mummification was a basic fact of Egyptian life. Commoners were mummified and placed in mass tombs, sometimes hundreds to each tomb. Having no riches to be plundered, some of these mummies are in better shape than the Pharaohs' mummies.

In fact, during the New Kingdom, no one wanted a fancy tomb anymore. Although impressive, the pyramids and necropolises did nothing but attract grave robbers who never had any respect for the dead. They often destroyed mummies trying to get to the treasure and gold.

So the Egyptian royalty found a new resting place, in the Valley of the Kings. This vast cemetery was an unpopulated mountain region west of Thebes (now called Luxor). Here, the complicated tunnels and passages were carved out of solid rock. The entrances were kept small and made to look like part of the mountains. Amenhotep I and Thutmose I were the first Pharaohs to have their tombs totally hidden.

Grave robbers still had the upper hand, though. The only tomb in the Valley of the Kings to be discovered undisturbed was the burial chamber of King Tutankhamen. That is why King Tut, who was a teenager and

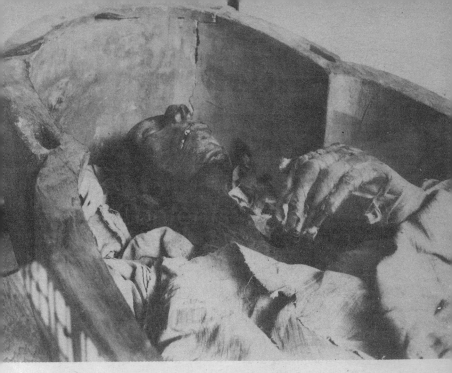

Rameses II was a popular Pharaoh who ruled from 1292 to 1225 B.C. Even if he could not be identified by other means, the distinctive crook of his nose would mark him as royalty. (The Bettmann Archive)

minor figure when he died, has become the most famous Pharaoh of all time.

Egyptian royalty were so desperate to protect their mummies from grave robbers that they started to do strange things. Pharaohs from earlier periods were taken from their big tombs and reburied in the Valley of the Kings. Later, kings and queens threw out the inhabitants of the best tombs and moved themselves in. The Pharaohs themselves became grave robbers, moving their ancestors' bones all around.

For example, Queen Hatshepsut liked her father's

15

tomb better than hers, so she moved Thutmose I into her tomb and took his. Rameses II was moved to the grave of Seti I, and then both mummies were moved to the vault of Queen Inhapi. The French archaeologist Victor Loret found a confusing sight: In Amenhotep II's tomb he found Amenhotep III's mummy, lying in Rameses III's sarcophagus. It was closed with the lid from Seti II's coffin!

So many reburials resulted in the discovery of two big collections of royal mummies. Queen Inhapi's tomb, discovered in 1881, was the resting place for 32 royal mummies and eight commoners. The royalty included Rameses II, III, and IX. The tomb Victor Loret discovered in 1898 contained 10 royal mummies and six unknown mummies. There lay the remains of Rameses IV, V, and VI, as well as Queen Tiye.

Most of the gold in the Valley of the Kings was lost long ago, but the mummies found there represent the highest achievement of the art. Specially trained priests spent 70 days working on each body. They learned to disinfect the body with palm wine and pad the flesh to make it even more lifelike.

The golden age of Egyptian mummy-making ended about 1085 B.C., when foreign rulers conquered Egypt and introduced their own funeral practices. Faithful priests kept up the practice for another 1000 years, but their results never measured up to the mummies of the New Kingdom.

In the Late and Greco-Roman Periods, the priests spent less time embalming the body and more time painting a portrait of the dead person on a wooden board that covered his face. With this lifelike mask, the spirits of the dead were able to find the right body even if it had decayed.

Egyptian mummy case from about 300 A.D. As the art of mummy-making declined, casket makers helped the spirits find their way to the body by painting a portrait of the deceased on the case. (The Bettmann Archive)

Spirits of the Dead

All of this was necessary because the Egyptians believed that each person had three spirits that lived on after death. They were called the *ka,* the *ba,* and the *chu.*

The ka was a person's double, what we might call his personality. The Pharaoh Thutmose III said his ka was like "a victorious bull who shone in the rings of Thebes." The ba was a bird-like spirit which liked to stay close to its "perch," the body it once lived in. The chu was a person's mind, or genius.

Each spirit had a different mission after its master's death. The ka was allowed to go in and out of the tomb and wander among the living, even eating and drinking, but it stayed on earth and lived forever in the tomb with its double. The ba had wings and flew with the sun on its nightly journey to the underworld, but it always returned to the tomb and the body. A body had to remain lifelike, or the ka and ba wouldn't be able to recognize it and return to it. Destruction of the body meant the loss of immortality. Only the chu went to the afterlife and stayed there.

The Egyptians left food, drink, jewelry, artwork, toys, and mummified pets in the tomb to make the ka feel at home. Poorer subjects made do with paintings of food, drink, and favorite belongings.

During the New Kingdom, the Egyptians believed in a fourth spirit, the *akh.* This spirit represented the dead person and was created during a strange ceremony called the Opening of the Mouth. Before the mummy was placed in the tomb, a relative or priest opened the mummy's mouth and called forth the akh.

According to the *Book of the Dead,* the akh journeyed to the underworld, where it was judged by the

The *Akh* is an Egyptian spirit that is released during the Opening of the Mouth ceremony. It flies to the underworld but always returns to the body in the tomb.
(The Bettmann Archive)

god Osiris. Dozens of beautiful amulets were buried with the mummy to help protect the akh on its journey. If it was judged worthy, the akh was allowed to live forever in the underworld with family and friends, which was the goal of every devout Egyptian.

The Egyptians also believed that a person's shadow and name were very important. If a person was judged to have lived a bad life, his shadow might be eaten by a horrible monster called the "shadow gobbler." To keep a person's name alive, his exploits were recorded in tomb paintings and carvings. As long as his name was

19

spoken by those who remembered him, it was believed he was immortal.

These ideas sound very strange to us today, but they evolved over many centuries. The Egyptians started out believing in a simple afterlife and a simple burial with a few clay pots. As they began to mummify their dead, the priests invented new religious ideas to explain the need for mummies. Mummification went hand-in-hand with religion, one serving to reinforce the other.

Chapter 3

King Tut's Curse
and Other Strange Stuff

Wings of Death

King Tut's tomb is famous because it is the only Pharaoh's tomb that had not been plundered by robbers before it was opened by archaeologists. Robbers tried to break in, but something scared them away before they could succeed. When the last chamber (the burial chamber) was opened by archaeologists in February, 1923, it was the first time anyone had entered that room since the teenage king was placed there 3272 years before.

The treasures found there have been exhibited all over the world. But the fascination with King Tut's tomb goes beyond its priceless artwork to the curse that is said to hang over the tomb.

In our modern age, people laugh at the idea of curses.

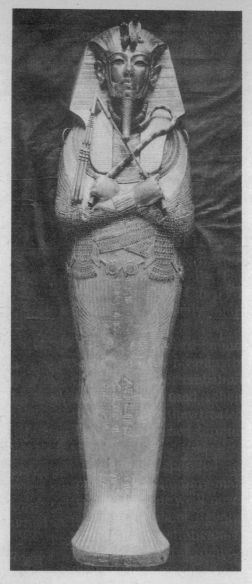

Tutankhamen's breathtaking golden burial mask is probably the most valuable ancient artifact ever found.
(The Metropolitan Museum of Art)

Impossible, they say. Who would believe that stuff? The ancient Egyptians believed strongly in magic, and every Pharaoh's court had its share of magicians. These were not the kind of magicians who pull rabbits out of hats—they conjured spells and curses.

Whether you believe in curses or not, something killed 22 people connected with the discovery of King Tutankhamen's tomb. Most died within a few months of opening the tomb; the rest were dead within six years. These people were not old and sick—they died in the prime of life!

A few died by accidents, but most of them died of a high fever, chills, and hallucinations. Many other people who explored Egyptian tombs also died of the same mysterious symptoms.

Did these people die from a curse? Or were they infected by things growing in the old, stale atmosphere of the tomb? Perhaps death wasn't caused by a curse or a disease—but by a deadly poison!

This strange story begins in 1907 when two Englishmen, Lord Carnarvon and Howard Carter, joined together to look for tombs in the Valley of the Kings. Carnarvon was a wealthy nobleman who had come to Egypt to escape the damp weather in England. Carter was a poor painter and archaeologist. Carnarvon had the money, and Carter had the knowledge.

An earlier explorer had uncovered pottery and a wooden chest mentioning a minor Pharaoh named Tutankhamen. All the tombs of the Pharoahs had been discovered except for this one, and Carter set out to look for it. For six years, he searched the Valley of the Kings. Carnarvon was ready to give up when Carter found some building stones near the tomb of Rameses VI. He believed the stones might mean the entrance to another tomb.

Lord Carnarvon was the wealthy Englishman who funded the search for King Tut's tomb in the 1920s. He was also the first to be struck down by the mysterious curse. (Ashmolean Museum, Oxford)

He was right, and things moved quickly after that. By November, 1922, they had found a door with the seals unbroken—an unheard-of occurrence—and soon the whole world was excited about their discovery. Like those of all the other Pharaohs, Tut's tomb had many chambers and passages, and it took the diggers until February, 1923, to explore the whole tomb.

In an outer chamber, they found a clay tablet that read:

Death will slay with his wings whoever disturbs the peace of the Pharaoh.

Carnarvon and Carter were disturbed because they didn't want the Egyptian workers to become afraid and stop working. They cataloged the tablet with the other artifacts, but it later disappeared. However, another curse appeared on the back of a statue in the main chamber. It read:

It is I who drive back the robbers of the tomb with the flames of the desert. I am the protector of Tutankhamen's grave.

By now, they had reached King Tut's burial chamber, and the Egyptian workers were no longer needed. Howard Carter himself chiseled through to the inner chamber, and he wrote later in *The Tomb of Tut-ankhamen* that, "We did not even want to break the seal, for a feeling of intrusion had descended heavily upon us . . . We felt we were in the presence of the dead king and must do him reverence."

Many important people were there at the opening of King Tut's burial chamber, and many more came in the days that followed. Most of them would be dead within a few years:

- Lord Carnarvon, whose money had funded the discovery, was the first to die. Less than six weeks after opening the tomb, he came down with a terrible fever, chills, and hallucinations. After twelve days of suffering, he died. Mysteriously, the electricity went out all over Cairo, and Lord Carnarvon's favorite dog died in London at the same time.

25

Carnarvon was 57 years old, and doctors said he infected himself while shaving.

- Arthur Mace, a famous American archaeologist who was present when the tomb was open, died a few days after Carnarvon in the same hotel. He fell into a deep coma, and doctors never decided what killed him.

- George Jay Gould was Carnarvon's best friend, and he came to see the discovery a few days after Carnarvon's death. Howard Carter took him into King Tut's tomb, and the next morning Gould fell prey to the same strange fever. By that night, he was dead. Doctors said it was bubonic plague.

- Joel Wool, another wealthy friend of Carnarvon's, went to see the tomb. He died aboard a ship a few days later while returning to England.

- Archibald Douglas Reid was the radiologist who cut the cords around King Tut and was the first person to X-ray the mummy. He soon came down with a strange disease that made him very weak, and he died in England a few months later.

- Lord Carnarvon's wife, Lady Almina, died in 1929, supposedly of an insect bite.

- Richard Bethell, who was Howard Carter's secretary and was present at the opening of the tomb, also died in 1929 of a lingering illness. His father leapt off a building that same day. Lastly, a little boy was killed when the hearse carrying Bethell's body ran over him on the way to the cemetery.

- James Breasted, a famous professor who had explored many tombs and was present when King Tut's was opened in 1923, did not die until 1935—but he died of the same mysterious fever after visiting King Tut's tomb again with Howard Carter.

26

All in all, 13 of the 20 people who were present at the opening of King Tut's burial chamber died within a few years. Nine more people who were connected with the discovery, like Carnarvon's wife and friends, also died. The dead included many famous professors and archaeologists, and newspapers of the day reported the curse as if it were real.

Oddly, Howard Carter did not die until 1939, at the age of 66. Carter probably explored more Egyptian tombs than anybody, and he often suffered from strange fevers and hallucinations. Could it be that King Tut's curse was really a disease, and that Howard Carter lived longer because he built up a resistance to it?

Curse, Fungus, or Poison?

Many theories have been offered to explain King Tut's curse. Some people say it was just a coincidence. But too many people have died of the same mysterious fever to call it that. More likely, King Tut's curse is the result of a long-lived disease or a magician's poison.

When King Tut's tomb was opened in 1923, the air in the burial chamber was 3272 years old and had never been disturbed. Fungus, a kind of microscopic plant, can live for hundreds of years in air like that. Another microscopic plant, bacteria, is found in all living and dead creatures. Both fungi and bacteria can cause terrible diseases. Were the people killed by something that was growing on the rotting mummy itself?

In 1962, an Egyptian medical doctor and biologist named Ezzeddin Taha announced that he had solved the curse. Many archaeologists reported labored breathing and strange skin irritations when they stayed in tombs too long; museum workers had exhibited similar symptoms after working with Egyptian artifacts. Taha believed that something was in that ancient dust.

He said it was a fungus called *Aspergillus niger*—able to survive in Egyptian tombs for 4000 years! When King Tut's burial chamber was first opened, the fungus was at its strongest and literally killed the first people who entered. It could take a couple of days or a couple of years, but sooner or later the fungus infected their lungs.

This theory was never proven, because a few weeks later Dr. Taha and his two closest aides died in a bizarre traffic accident on a road he traveled daily. Taha apparently had a heart attack and drove his car into a head-on collision. Many newspapers reported that King Tut's curse had struck again.

Dr. Taha was right about one thing: Doctors in the 1920s and 1930s didn't think about fungi. They laid the blame for the 22 deaths on bug bites, bubonic plague, pneumonia, and things they knew about. After Taha announced his theory, though, doctors all over the world started to look for similar cases—and found them, too.

In South Africa, a cave explorer nearly died of a fungal attack after entering a cave full of bats. Explorers of Incan caves in Peru told similar stories. Finally, it was proven that these cave exploreres had a disease named *histoplasmosis,* which is caused by an infectious fungus that lives in rotting matter. This sounds exactly like the theory offered by the dead Dr. Taha.

Parasites are also a possibility. A parasite is a creature that lives inside another living creature, like a tapeworm. Depending on the part of the body it attacks, a parasite can cause serious disease.

Before antibiotics, European miners and tunnel

28

workers suffered from a disease caused by hookworms and threadworms. Like fungi, these parasites entered the body through dust in the air and grew inside the miners' lungs. This parasitic attack was so common that it earned the nickname "Tunnel Disease."

Parasites and fungi make the curse sound as if it occurred naturally, instead of supernaturally. There's also a third possibility: Lord Carnarvon and the others were poisoned.

The Egyptians were expert poisoners—they knew about hemlock, arsenic, opium, and many other poisons. They perfected the deadly poison called aconite, which is made from an herb called monkshood. A thimbleful of aconite can kill a man. The Pharaoh Menes kept a garden of poisonous herbs, and Queen Cleopatra was said to be the greatest poisoner of all.

Priests knew how to extract poison from snakes and scorpions. There is evidence that they gave themselves small doses of poison in order to hallucinate during religious festivals.

Doctors had antidotes for known poisons. According to ancient medical records, the remedy for scorpion poison was honey and hippopotamus droppings.

Hallucinations, rapid heart failure, breathing problems, and weakness are all symptoms of poisoning. It has been proven that poison-tipped arrows are still deadly after hundreds of years. Some poisons could easily last thousands of years.

Priests and court magicians had complete control over the royal mummies, and they often operated in secret. They had plenty of time to coat the sarcophagus and the bandages with poison. When the coffin was opened, the dried poison could float out with the dust and infect all who breathed the air.

29

If this was the case, why didn't everyone who entered Tut's tomb die? People have different reactions to poison—the same amount might kill one person and not affect another at all. In addition, the more often a person went into the tomb, the more poison entered his system.

We may never have the opportunity to apply modern scientific techniques to the mystery of King Tut's Curse, because no unopened Pharaoh's tomb has been discovered since King Tut's. It's certain that if another one is found, the explorers will be wearing oxygen tanks and protective suits when they enter, but that won't save them if it's a supernatural curse.

An explorer named Engelbach discovered another scary curse in a tomb near the Great Pyramids:

The spirit of the dead will wring the neck of a grave robber as if it were that of a goose.

Mummy Medicine

With the possibility of poison, fungi, and bacteria growing all over a mummy, you probably wouldn't want to touch one. So how would you like to *eat* a mummy? At one time, people actually swallowed ground-up mummy as medicine!

For many centuries, mummy was one of the most highly prized medicines in the world. Every drugstore, called an apothecary, had a big jar of mummy powder. They were happy to sell customers a scoop or two. Doctors prescribed it for everything from whooping cough to broken bones. Mummy was good for one thing—swallowing too much of it almost always brought on vomiting.

The craze of "mummy medicine" started during the Middle Ages when people began taking the embalming chemical, bitumen, as a medicine. Persian mummies contained some bitumen, and they were worth more than Egyptian mummies. Soon people were determined to take mummy for all of their ills, and they didn't care where it came from. "Mummy factories" sprang up all over Egypt to find—or make—mummies.

Thousands, maybe millions, of priceless mummies were stolen from tombs and ground up for medicine. When the real mummies began to run out, the factories substituted any dead bodies they could find. Unscrupulous mummy dealers took recent bodies, covered them in rags and asphalt, dried them in the sun, and sold them as real mummies.

Mummy hands, feet, and other pieces fetched high prices. Some people wanted to grind their mummy themselves to make sure they got the real thing.

In the 1700s, Egypt finally got so worried about losing mummies they clamped down on the gruesome business. People got worried that mummy powder was fake, and they found new drugs. Today, in certain parts of the world, it's rumored that enough money will still buy you the real thing!

Animal Mummies

Before the X-ray machine became reliable, dozens of museums had collected what they thought were Egyptian child mummies. The little bundles were certainly the right shape and size. After they started X-raying them, they were amazed to find almost all the child mummies were really baboons.

The Egyptians had a thriving business in mummify-

Cat mummies, three of thousands discovered in Egyptian galleries of animal mummies. Cats were sacred to the cat-headed goddess, Bast.

(The British Museum)

ing animals as well as humans. In addition to baboons, they mummified cats, dogs, birds, crocodiles, lizards, snakes, scorpions, fish, and even hippopotami!

These were all animals that were sacred to the Egyptians. For example, crocodiles were sacred to the god Sebek. The historian Herodotus reported seeing a pool of sacred crocodiles with bejeweled feet. Birds honored the bird-headed god Horus, keeper of the morning sun. Dogs were sacred in some cities and eaten in others.

Crocodile mummy. Crocodiles were sacred to the god Sebek, who had a crocodile's head himself.
(The Metropolitan Museum of Art)

One animal that was mummified because he literally *was* a god was the Apis Bull. A group of devout Egyptians worshipped a living bull who had special markings, including a white diamond between his eyes. This cult thought the bull was born of the goddess Isis and represented the very first god. When they found such a bull, they took him to their temple and treated him like royalty. When an Apis Bull died, he was mummified with the care given a king or a high priest.

Almost all the Apis Bulls were buried together in a huge tomb at Saqqara. Only a few animals were buried with humans—most had their own special tombs. For example, thousands of baboons and large birds, called ibises, were stored in special galleries at Tuna el Gebel.

Most of the cat and dog mummies were undoubtedly pets, but it's unlikely that many Egyptians kept ferocious adult baboons as pets. The large number of animal mummies suggests that most were bred to become mummies. They were probably manufactured in advance and sold to people as tomb offerings. If someone wanted a hippopotamus mummy, he didn't wait for a hippo to die—he bought a mummy.

More Mummy Products

The mummy business has kept lots of people employed, from priests who made mummies to quacks who made mummy powder 3000 years later. To some people, a mummy wasn't worth nearly as much as its bandages.

The mummy of Pharaoh Rameses III was wrapped in 350 yards of the finest linen. One hundred and fifty yards of linen was common for an Egyptian mummy. For centuries, Bedouin nomads collected mummies in the desert, cleaned the bandages, and sold them as rag paper. They were the first to make paper from mummies, but they weren't the last.

Augustus Stanwood, a U.S. paper manufacturer, thought it would be a good idea to make high-quality paper from mummy wrappings. In the late 1800s, he imported a bunch of mummies to his paper mill in Maine. The first batch was stained dark from embalming resins, and Stanwood had to make brown wrapping paper out of them. Another batch caused an epidemic of cholera, a deadly disease, and Stanwood was forced to close his business.

34

Stanwood had probably gotten a supply of fake mummies, people who had died recently from cholera. Cases like this only increased the superstitions about mummies. It's sad that so many mummies were lost for such silly reasons. They must have been plentiful at one time.

Mark Twain, the creator of Tom Sawyer and Huck Finn, told about riding an Egyptian train in his book *Innocents Abroad*. He said the engineers were tossing mummies into the boiler, burning them like logs.

According to Twain, one of the men complained, "Damn these plebeians, they don't burn worth a cent! Pass out a king!"

Chapter 4

How to Make
an Egyptian Mummy

Many ancient cultures mummified their dead, but when we think of mummies, we usually think only of Egyptian mummies. For 3000 years, the inhabitants of the Valley of the Kings have haunted our dreams and our nightmares.

This isn't accidental. The Egyptians intended for their mummies to last forever. The steps they performed to create a mummy are incredible and could not be duplicated today. Luckily, the Egyptians kept good records and were visited by many historians, such as Herodotus. We don't know everything, but we have a good idea how the Egyptians made a mummy.

So pretend you are an Egyptian priest in training. Like your father and grandfather before you, you will learn the ancient arts and secrets. You will spend 70 days—almost two-and-a-half months—working on a single mummy. When you are done, you will have made a lasting home for the spirits of the dead.

Preparations for Death

Long before he died, an Egyptian began making plans for his death. A Pharaoh might start building his tomb the day he came to power. A high priest or a member of the Pharaoh's family would be guaranteed royal treatment and a resting place near the king. Merchants and other commoners got as much as they could pay for.

Herodotus visited Egypt about 500 B.C. Mummy-making was still common, but the quality had slipped a little. At that time, natron was the most important chemical used to dry the body. Natron is a combination of sodium bicarbonate and sodium chloride (or sodium sulfate). Natron is like salt and is found at the bottom of dry lake beds.

Much of what Herodotus saw in Egypt was verified by another Greek historian, Diodorus Siculus. They both said there were three different ways to make a mummy, depending on how much money a person could spend. A customer was shown examples of the three different methods and asked to choose which one he wanted.

The cheapest way was chosen by poor people. In this process, the internal organs were not removed. Instead, the stomach and intestines were flushed out with liquids, much like a mechanic flushes the radiator of a car. Then the body was covered with natron and other chemicals and left to "cure" for 70 days. Then it was handed over to the relatives for burial in a mass tomb.

An adult and child mummy were found together in a tomb that is typical of the graves of non-royalty.
(The Bettmann Archive)

This was a cheap Egyptian funeral, but it would be impossible to find an undertaker who would go to this much trouble today.

The mid-price method was a little more complicated. The organs were still not removed, but the body was filled with cedar oil. This was done with syringes, like the kind the doctor uses to give you a shot when you're sick. The oil was left inside the body for 70 days, where it dissolved most of the internal organs. Meanwhile, the outside of the body was dried with natron.

After 70 days, deep punctures were made in the body, and the oil seeped out, taking what was left of the organs with it. Removal of the organs was very important, because internal organs always decompose first. The Egyptians knew that if the organs were removed and the remaining flesh was dried out, a body could last forever.

The third and most expensive way to make a mummy was very complicated. It was reserved for royalty, priests, and wealthy Egyptians.

Royal Treatment

The process of mummy-making began with a death. When an important man died, the women of his house—his wife, mother, daughters, sisters—started to scream. When their neighbors heard the screams, they knew someone had died.

The women showed their grief to all. They put mud on their heads and walked through the streets with their breasts bared. They cried, beat their chests, and called the name of the dead man. The men of the family walked behind them, also shouting and beating their bare chests.

A quieter parade followed this, when the relatives took the dead man to the embalmer's shop. Priests followed the body, chanting prayers to the dead man.

The embalmers often worked in a tent, because the work was hot and involved dangerous chemicals. If they worked in a regular building, the fumes from the chemicals might overcome them. To avoid the heat, they often worked at night.

Priests were in charge of mummification. These priests not only shaved their heads, they shaved *all* of the hair off their bodies. The chief priest represented the god Anubis and wore a jackal mask. The jackal is an animal like a wolf, so he looked very frightening. While the embalmers did the hard work, the priests performed rituals and burned incense.

Here are the steps the priests and embalmers performed to make a mummy:

1. They bathed the body and laid it out on a high table, so they wouldn't have to bend over.

2. They removed the dead man's brain by inserting a long hook-like instrument into his nose and scooping out the brain in little pieces. Experts did this difficult work, because one wrong move could damage the man's face. They used chemicals to remove any remaining brain parts.

3. With great ritual, the chief priest painted a line on the left side of the dead body. This line was about five inches long and showed where the body was to be cut open in the next step.

4. Another expert was brought in. Using a sharp knife called an Ethiopian Stone, he cut a hole in the body where the line was. Then he reached in and carefully removed all the internal organs. Sometimes the heart was left in the body, because it was the center of knowledge.

   Taking out the organs was hard work, and the man who did it had to be very strong. He was also considered unclean, and the others would chase him out of the tent when he was done.

5. Once removed, the stomach, liver, lungs, and intestines were mummified separately and placed

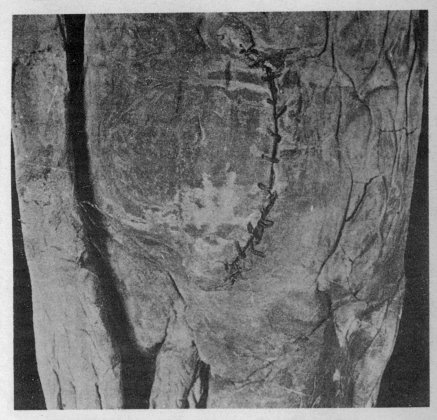

This Egyptian mummy shows the traditional incision that was made in the body to remove the internal organs. (The Bettmann Archive)

in special jars called canopic jars. A jar shaped like a man's head held the stomach, and the intestines were put in a jar shaped like a dog's head. The lungs went into a jackal-headed jar, and the liver was placed in a jar shaped like a hawk's head. The lids of the jars were then sealed with wax.

Sometimes, the mummified organs were put back into the body. As we will see later, these mummified organs have proven very valuable to modern scientists.

6. The main torso of the body was now empty, and the embalmers washed it out with palm wine. They rubbed it with perfumes, such as myrrh and cassia. The wine and perfume not only made the mummy smell good, they were also good preservatives.

7. It was time for the padding. The empty torso was stuffed with linen soaked in resin, a natural glue. Some mummies, especially women, had padding put under their skin to keep it lifelike. This worked well with some mummies but not so well with others, when the padding distorted the face.

8. The body was now ready for drying. It was placed on a special sloping table and covered with natron powder. For over two months, the body was dried by chemicals and the sun. This and the removal of the organs were the crucial parts of mummy-making.

9. When the skin was dry and hard as old leather, it was time to prepare the mummy for wrapping. The body was bathed and then rubbed with spices, herbs, and perfumes. The mouth, eyes, and nose were cleaned, stuffed with linen, and sealed with wax. Thin wires of gold were fastened around the

dead man's fingernails and toenails to keep them from falling out.

The embalmers sewed up the hole where the organs had been removed, and the priests sealed it with a special plate that bore a sacred symbol called the Eye of Horus. Even today, we still use this eye symbol on our dollar bills.

10. Now the mummy was wrapped in the finest linen—between 150 and 350 yards. The wrapping went on for several days, and there were many rituals. The Egyptians themselves didn't know what strange rituals the priests performed on a body, and as we said earlier, some mummies may have been covered with poison in order to "curse" tomb robbers.

Amulets and jewelry were placed inside the wrappings to protect the dead man on his trip to the underworld. Rings were placed on his fingers, and golden earrings were hung in his ears. Finally, the wrapped mummy was coated in resin, which hardened like varnish.

11. While all this was going on, artists were busy making the beautiful coffins that would house the mummy. His relatives collected food, furniture, and other belongings his spirits would need in the afterlife. After 70 days, it was time for the funeral.

Immortality

Egyptians prepared well for death. By the time an important person died, his tomb had already been built. Perhaps it had been decided he would share a tomb with relatives or other nobility. A priest might be buried with other priests, for example. Members of the Pharaoh's court might be buried in the necropolis outside the Pharaoh's tomb.

Arrangements were made with the ka priest to make sure the mummy got fresh food and drink. (As we read before, the ka was the spirit that stayed with the mummy in his tomb.) The ka went on enjoying food, drink, and personal belongings. If the belongings included valuable treasure, the ka priest might also arrange for armed men to guard the tomb.

The funeral began by placing the mummy in his mummiform coffin. This was a small coffin that was painted to look like the dead man.

Then the procession to the tomb began. First came a parade of priests and priestesses dressed as gods in masks shaped like animal heads. Then came the mummy in a beautiful wagon, called a bier, which was pulled by men and oxen. This was followed by a smaller bier that held the canopic jars containing the internal organs.

Members of the dead man's family trailed behind the biers, again crying and beating their breasts in sorrow. It was a very long walk to the tomb, and some of them fainted and were carried by servants. The servants also carried the toilet articles, furniture, jewelry, and other goods that would be buried with the mummy. If this was a poor man's funeral, these objects might be painted on the tomb's walls instead.

At the entrance to the tomb, priests and relatives performed the Opening of the Mouth ceremony. They stuck a carpenter's tool called an *adze* into the mummy's mouth to free the spirit called the akh. The akh would go to the underworld to be judged by Osiris.

The priests performed many other rituals and burned much incense. The ceremonies could take many hours. Finally, the priests carried the mummy into the tomb and sealed it within the large sarcophagus. No one came with them, because they didn't want people to know how the tomb was built.

After the service, everyone went back to the dead man's house and had a great feast. There were musicians and dancers, and they all sang songs to the dead man. Sadness was over, and it was time to celebrate his immortality!

Chapter 5

Mummies from Around the World

The ancient Egyptians did not have a monopoly on mummies, so how did this strange practice develop among societies that couldn't possibly have known one another?

There are some theories that the Canary Islands were settled by Egyptians, who brought the practice of mummification with them, but it's unlikely that they ever visited Peru or Russia. More likely, these people all observed accidental mummies in caves and pits, as we have, and that gave them the idea.

They used whatever natural resources they had to preserve the body: heat, cold, tree gum, lime, salt, even smoke. Most of them learned that bodies lasted longer when the internal organs were removed. They also developed complex religious and cultural practices to go along with mummification.

More mummies would exist from ancient times if later conquerors, like the Spaniards, hadn't destroyed them. The saddest example of all is the Incas of Peru.

Incan Mummies

Mummy-making in Peru and northern Chile goes back at least 5000 years—earlier than the Egyptians. In these pre-Incan days, mummies were sewn, sitting up, in simple sacks. The mummies inside the sacks often did not have heads, so a doll's head or a captured human head decorated the top of the bundle.

We'll never know why so many of these mummies had false heads instead of real ones. Maybe they lost them in battle, or maybe their relatives took the heads home and kept them as souvenirs. Many of the pre-Incan mummy bundles had small dolls sewn all over them. These were probably good luck charms to ward off evil spirits.

When the Spaniards arrived in Peru about 1530 A.D., there were no simple settlements anymore. Instead, there was a vast empire that stretched for 3000 miles along the entire western coast of South America. Little is known about how the Incan empire evolved from its humble beginnings, because the Incas did not leave written records like the Egyptians.

The Incas were great builders; they erected incredible cities, palaces, and temples from stone. Their city-states were linked by roads and a thriving economy. They were accomplished farmers and grew corn, potatoes, fruits, beans, and grains on large plantations that were terraced and irrigated. They mined gold, silver, tin, and copper and made beautiful jewelry. These golden orna-

Pre-Incan mummy. Most South American mummies were buried sitting up in a sturdy mummy sack.
(The Bettmann Archive)

ments proved to be their downfall, because the Spaniards were willing to kill for gold.

The Spaniards were also fascinated by Incan mummies and funeral practices. They observed the Incas and traded with them for some time before they conquered them. Almost everything we know about the Incas comes from Spanish reports.

Death Only the Beginning

After death, every Inca was mummified and dressed in his finest clothes for burial. Like the pre-Incan mummies, the Incas were mummified sitting down. Embalming methods varied from one part of the empire to another, but they usually started by removing the internal organs.

In the dry desert and coastal areas, bodies were preserved by burying them in the sand or leaving them in the sun. In the damper mountain climates, the bodies were hung over fires in caves and smoked until they were dry. Some Incas used herbs to dry out the body and turn it into a mummy.

Special attention was given to the royal mummies. After mummification, a dead king was not buried but was dressed in his finest robes and placed on his throne. His favorite servants, wives, and llamas were sacrificed to show their sorrow. The dead king was placed in his litter and carried through the streets while his subjects wailed and moaned. (The "litter" in this case refers to a covered and curtained couch that is made to be carried.) In the capital city of Cuzco, the mummy might be taken to the house of his relatives and offered food and drink.

Eventually, the royal mummy ended up in a special tomb where he would sit with other royal mummies. They were brought fresh food, drink, weapons, and clothing, and the reigning king would come to ask their advice. During holidays and religious festivals, the royal mummies were dressed in new clothing and paraded through the streets. The crowds cheered and treated them as if they were still alive.

We know about these practices from the Spanish reports, but we don't know much about the Incas' religious beliefs. However, they must have believed strongly in an afterlife to mummify everyone and leave food, drink, and belongings for the mummies to enjoy.

Sadly, the Spaniards decided that trading with the Incas was not enough. They wanted all their gold. They conquered the Incas, massacred tens of thousands of them, and forced the rest to work as slaves in the mines they once owned. Because the Spaniards believed the royal mummies represented a pagan religion, they burned every one they could find. There are reports of distraught natives gathering up the ashes of their beloved kings to worship as before.

The only Incan mummies that survive today are the mummies of commoners that the Spaniards didn't bother with. Still, scientists have learned a great deal by studying these long-dead residents of South America. The same thing happened, on a lesser scale, with the Guanches of the Canary Islands.

Guanche Mummies

Americans know very little about the seven Canary Islands, which lie off the west coast of Africa, but they are a popular stop for European vacationers. Grand Canary, Tenerife, Lanzarote, Fuerteventura, La Palma, Gomera, and Hierro are provinces of Spain now, but thousands of years ago they were home to an unusual race of people who mummified their dead.

From all accounts, the Guanches (pronounced *Wonchez*) were a race of tall, strong people with red or blonde hair—very different from the Hispanic people who live there today. One theory is that they were descended from Vikings, the great warrior-sailors from Northern Europe. Some say they were Egyptians. The most romantic theory is that the Canary Islands are the remnants of the lost civilization of Atlantis.

The islands are near where Homer and others described Atlantis as being, "beyond the Pillars of Hercules." (Today we call the "Pillars of Hercules" the Straits of Gibraltar.) Ancient historians Plato and Plutarch even went so far as to call these islands the Atlantides. They have always been very isolated, bounded by the Western Sahara on one side and thousands of miles of water on every other side.

The Guanche civilization lasted over 3500 years, from about 2000 B.C. to almost 1600 A.D., when they were conquered by the Spaniards. The islanders had no gunpowder, but they were deadly accurate with their slings and spears. It took the Spanish conquistadors almost 300 years it defeat them, island by island. Most of the Guanches were massacred or taken for slaves; the rest intermarried with the conquerors. No Guanche descendants are alive today.

Because the Guanches lived in caves, they seemed primitive to the Spaniards, but their culture was very complex. For example, when the population grew too large, men and women walked on separate paths as a

51

form of natural birth control. The Guanches communicated over great distances by means of a whistling language, and they worshipped a supreme god who went by a different name on each island.

The Guanches were so skilled at preserving bodies that some six-foot-tall mummies weigh only six or seven pounds. Like the Egyptians, they started the mummification process by removing the internal organs. This was cursed work performed by outcasts. The actual embalmers were priests or priestesses, and they only worked on members of their own sex.

After the organs were removed, they coated the body inside and out with the dark red resin of the dragon's-blood tree. Some dragon's-blood trees are over 3000 years old, and their gum is still used as a preservative. The mummy was then covered with straw mats and sewn inside several sheepskins or goatskins.

If the dead man was a king, he was buried in a deep cave shaft, and only the priests knew the location. Sometimes a king's mummy was left unburied for years, so that his spirit could advise the new king. Kings were buried standing up, and their wives were buried lying on their sides.

Like the Incas, the Guanches mummified almost everyone. They buried commoners in layers, one on top of another. Male mummies always had their arms at their sides, and female mummies had their arms folded. Jugs of milk and butter and bowls of figs and dried fruit were left with the mummies in case their spirits got hungry.

The Spaniards reported only what they saw and never tried to learn much about the Guanches and their beliefs, so the mummies and a few artifacts are all that remain of these mysterious people. Guanche mummies can be seen in such museums as the Canary Islands Museum in Las Palmas, Grand Canary.

Scythian Mummies

The Scythians were nomads who wandered the plains of Siberia and Outer Mongolia 2000 to 3000 years ago. Nomads are people who constantly move from place to place, instead of settling down. The Scythians were like early Russian cowboys, riding horses behind great herds of goats and sheep. Whole tribes wandered with the herds, every man, woman, and child doing his or her share of the work.

According to the Greek historian Herodotus, the Scythians were fierce horsemen and warriors. They raided Greek and Persian outposts and took what they wanted. Most importantly, these proud people revered their chiefs and nobles and mummifed them with as much skill as the Egyptians.

Like the Egyptians, the Scythians first removed the dead person's brain, and almost all Scythian mummies have a hole chiseled just behind the ear for its removal. They removed the rest of the major organs, like the stomach and heart, and then salted the inside of the body.

The Scythians made one major improvement over the Egyptians: they slit the dead person's arms and legs, took out his muscles, stuffed the arms and legs with grass or horsehair, and then sewed them back up. This sounds grotesque, but the muscles were one less thing inside the body to decay. The Scythians also had the cold climate of Siberia and Outer Mongolia to help them make mummies.

Some of the Scythian practices were also similar to those of the Incas. After embalming a king's body, they covered it with wax and paraded it throughout the kingdom for 40 days. At every stop, the men of that area would cut their hair short, slice off a piece of their ear, and push an arrow through their left hand. The king's wife and servants were often put to death, along with his horses, and sometimes the horses were mummified.

Scythian graves were covered loosely with boulders, which allowed cold air to enter and finish the mummification process. Their clothing—soft leather pants and boots, and wool tunics and stockings—was also preserved by the cold. We wish we knew more about these proud nomads who wandered the Russian plains on horseback, but only their well-dressed mummies remain.

Capuchin Mummies

Not all mummies are thousands of years old, and not all mummies are made by the traditional method of removing the organs and drying the body. Some are just put into a cave and left to mummify on their own, such as the Capuchin mummies of Sicily.

For centuries, monks of the Capuchin order have lived in monasteries on the rocky island of Sicily, off the coast of Italy. (A monk is a very religious person who gives up the world we know to farm and clean and live a simple life, spending most of his time praying.) Centuries ago, they discovered a large cave where the climate was very dry and cold.

Coldness and dryness are two of the best conditions to have to make a mummy. About two hundred years

**Capuchin monks keep hanging around for centuries
after they die in the famous cemetery in Palermo,
Sicily, off the coast of Italy.** (UPI/Bettmann)

ago, the monks began putting their dead into the cave, also called a catacomb. They leaned them against the wall or laid them down on bunkbeds, still wearing their monk robes. Soon, the villagers who lived nearby asked if they could put their dead into the monks' cave. The monks agreed.

Today, the Cave of the Capuchins contains the mummies of over 8000 men, women, and children who died over a hundred years ago. All of the mummies are very well-preserved and dressed in their best clothes. The catacomb is now a famous tourist attraction, although not everyone wants to see 8000 recent mummies.

Other Cave Mummies

Cave mummies have been found all over the world, from China to Eastern Europe to the United States. Kentucky, Tennessee, Arizona, and Wyoming all have caves where Native Americans placed their dead to be mummified. Mammoth Cave in Kentucky contains limestone deposits that helped to preserve the Indian bodies stored there.

One of the largest collection of cave mummies is in the Mexican city of Guanajuato. High up in the mountains with a dry climate, the entire city is like a tomb. The dead are placed in tiers above ground, where they dry out and become mummies. After a certain time, they are moved to an underground chamber to make room for the newly dead.

Tourists like to visit Guanajuato, but the real purpose of the mummies is to allow villagers to visit all of their dead relatives.

The Aleut Eskimos of the remote Aleutian Islands

also buried their dead in caves. Many of these bodies were mummified by a combination of cold air and dry heat, which came from volcanic activity deep in the earth. Reports from explorers in the year 1790 suggested that the Aleuts also embalmed their dead by removing the organs and filling the bodies with dried hay and grass.

Cave mummies were created by natural conditions, but they were usually placed in the caves on purpose. There is, however, a whole class of mummies that were formed entirely by accident. The most famous of them are called the Bog People.

The high mountain air of Mexico is famous for its mummifying qualities. These monks and nuns have lasted hundreds of years in a Carmelite monastery in San Angel. (The Bettmann Archive)

Chapter 6

Bog People
and Ice Mummies

Have you ever seen a pond that is so full of brown muck that it looks thick, like soup? That is how a bog begins—moss and other plants decay in a pond or lake for centuries until the water dries up. What's left is called peat. Peat bogs are common all over Northern Europe, from England to Russia. Because the peat has carbonized it will burn, and the people of those countries dig it up, dry it out, and use it for fuel.

Sometimes, however, peat cutters dug up more than they expected! Over 600 natural mummies have been found in peat bogs, mainly in Denmark, England, and Germany. The peat contains lots of acid but no oxygen, and the bodies are preserved like leather. The carbon in the peat turns them black. Scientists call this group of accidental mummies the Bog People.

The oldest bog mummies date from the Iron Age,

about 2000 years ago. Most of Northern Europe at that time was settled by a people called Celts. According to the Romans, who fought them and traded with them, the Celts did not normally throw their dead into lakes or bogs. They burned them on raised platforms, called funeral pyres, or buried them in the ground.

Being thrown into a bog was special treatment. Even more curious is the fact that the oldest Bog People had all been hanged, strangled, or otherwise murdered.

Because bogs start out as lakes and ponds, it is believed that some people may have fallen in while getting a drink or walking too close to the edge. However, many Bog People still have the ropes that killed them around their necks. The mystery is whether they were hanged as punishment for crimes—or sacrificed to appease the gods.

Tollund Man

On May 8, 1950, in a bog near Aarhus, Denmark, diggers came upon a body seven feet down. It was so well-preserved that they called the police, thinking a murder had been committed. It was only after a local professor took the body to the Danish National Museum in Copenhagen that they learned it was about 2000 years old.

Tollund Man, as he was called after the name of the bog, was naked except for a leather hat, a belt, and a rope around his neck. He had been hanged or strangled, that was sure, but there was no other sign of violence. His face was peaceful and serene.

Tollund Man may have worn a linen gown that had rotted away, but his belt, cap, and noose were of fine

Tollund Man was discovered in a peat bog in Denmark, and has been dated to have died over 2000 years ago. Notice his leather cap, belt, and the rope around his neck. (The National Museum of Denmark)

workmanship. Still in his stomach were the remains of his last meal of spring grains and flower seeds. That strange meal and the man's peaceful expression led the researchers to believe that he had been sacrificed. They guessed that Tollund Man was a priest who had volunteered to die to ensure a fertile harvest.

Lindow Man

The most recently discovered bog mummy goes further to prove the religious connection. Lindow Man was discovered in 1984 in a bog near Cheshire, England. He was not as well-preserved as Tollund Man, having been accidentally cut in half by peat diggers, and his face was squashed. But an examination of Lindow Man's stomach told scientists a great deal.

By 1984, methods to examine food in a dead person's stomach had improved, thanks to the work of coroners. Forensic tests were performed on Lindow Man, and the coroners determined that he had eaten a piece of fresh bread that had been smudged with charcoal on the bottom. Right after eating the bread, he had been bashed on the head, strangled, and had his throat slit.

He died at about the same time and under the same conditions as Tollund Man, who lived across the sea in Denmark. Little is known about the Danish Celts, but much is known about the English Celts, thanks to the Romans. Like the Spaniards, the Romans were fond of writing about the people they were trying to conquer. From their reports, we know that English Celts had a priestly class called the Druids, and the Druids practiced human sacrifice.

Two thousand years ago, most of the world practiced

human sacrifice. The Romans, who acted horrified at the idea, were the same ones who threw Christians to the lions for amusement. The Druids eagerly accepted death, if it blessed the crops and made the land fertile. Lindow Man was probably killed during the spring fertility festival, Beltain, which occurs on May 1.

The burnt bread is important, because that was how a priest was chosen to die. Many small loaves of bread were baked, but only one of them was smudged on the bottom. He who chose the burnt bread was selected. His friends killed him quickly and made sure he was dead before they dropped him in the water.

Like Tollund Man, Lindow Man seemed to have lived an easy life for those primitive times. He was in good health and about 30 years old, which was the favorite age for a sacrificial victim. Also, there were no signs that he struggled against his death. Lindow Man was probably a very respected priest who picked the wrong piece of bread.

Condemned to Die

Not all Bog People went peacefully to their deaths. Three mummies were found in another Danish bog not far from where Tollund Man was found. The horrible expressions on their faces and the way their bodies were treated show they were probably hanged as punishment.

They are called the Borremose mummies after the name of a nearby town. A peat cutter found the first Borremose body in 1946. In addition to being hanged, he had had his skull crushed and a tree limb had been tied to his naked body to keep it from floating to the

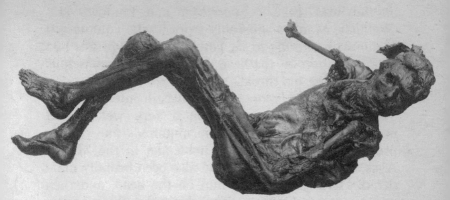

Borremose Man is another famous bog person from Denmark. For some reason, the feet are usually the best preserved part of bog people.
(The National Museum of Denmark)

surface. This mummy dates from about 840 B.C., making him one of the oldest Bog People.

The second Borremose body was found the next year, about a half-mile from the first. This female corpse is almost 400 years newer than Borremose Man and dates from 475 B.C. Sadly, near the body, there were some small bones belonging to a baby. Perhaps a mother and her child were thrown into the bog together.

The third body was found in 1948 and was also the body of a woman, but her face had been smashed, and she had been scalped before being thrown into the bog. The scalp of hair was found just a few inches above her head. Her body was dated to 770 B.C., proving that Borremose must have been a thriving village for a long time.

Grauballe Man was the last ancient mummy found in Denmark, and he hails from about 55 B.C. He died from having his throat slit, although he had also been clubbed on the head. Like Tollund Man and Lindow Man, Grauballe Man was probably a priest who volunteered to die as an offering to the gods. His fellow priests had kindly hit him on the head, making him unconscious before slitting his throat.

Some finds are more recent but still interesting. In Sweden, a farmer came upon a very well-dressed mummy in his peat bog. The mummy's fine clothes proved that he had been a nobleman in the Middle Ages, about 1350 A.D. He had also been brutally murdered. His murderers hit him on the head, and then drove a wooden stake through his heart. They apparently wanted to make sure he stayed dead!

Many Bog People have been found in Germany, and most of them exhibit signs of punishment. A 14-year-old girl had been put in the bog wearing a blindfold, and her hair had been shaved off on one side of her head. The body of a middle-aged man was found nearby, and he appeared to have been strangled with a hickory stick.

Probably thousands of bodies were found in bogs before modern science began to study them, but until this century, people who found a body in a bog would rebury it. Out of respect for the dead, they took the body to a cemetery and gave it a proper funeral. Those Bog People have been lost, but we still have the hope of finding more!

Ice Mummies

In 1972, the frozen body of an Eskimo woman appeared along the shore of Saint Lawrence Island in the Bering Sea. Scientists were surprised to find that the woman died about 400 A.D. and had been preserved in

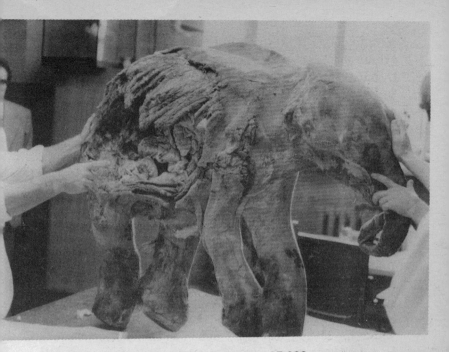

This baby mammoth was frozen over 27,000 years ago in Siberia, Russia. It is the oldest mummy ever to be discovered in such good condition. (UPI/Bettmann)

ice for almost 1600 years! An earthquake or landslide had probably destroyed her house and buried her under tons of ice. A sudden thawing released her body from its frozen tomb.

The Eskimo woman was so well-preserved that scientists could study the tattoos on her skin and tell what diseases she suffered from.

The most amazing frozen mummy ever discovered, however, was not human—it was a young woolly mammoth that died over 27,000 years ago. The mammoth is a long-extinct ancestor of the elephant, and such a complete specimen had never been found before. Shaggy fur still clung to its thick legs. The poor baby had probably wandered off from its mother and fallen into a crevice, where a glacier preserved it for thousands of years.

Russian gold prospectors found the baby mammoth in Siberia in 1977, and were able to refrigerate it before it decayed. For centuries, there have been reports of frozen human and animal mummies being discovered in cold areas—but none remain. Unlike mummies dried by deserts or embalming, frozen mummies can decay quickly after being exposed to normal sunlight and heat. If they are left in the wild, they are often eaten by scavengers, such as wolves and vultures.

We may never know how many frozen mummies have been accidentally destroyed, or how many still lie under the ice; the vast glaciers of this planet may hold wonders we can only dream about.

Chapter 7

Movie Mummies

One place where mummies really are immortal is in the movies. For most of us, the first mummy we ever saw was on TV in some old movie. There he was: a gnarly face, moldy bandages hanging off his body, shuffling after a pretty girl. A mummy like that may be fun and even a little scary, but it's total make-believe.

In real life, there is no possibility of any mummy getting up and walking around. You can be sure that after a person has his brain and internal organs removed, he isn't going anywhere.

We can't blame Hollywood for showing mummies that aren't realistic. They look so lifelike that it's easy to imagine they could come back to life; they're thousands of years old and come from the mysterious past. They're also found in spooky tombs, which always look neat in the movies. Besides, a mummy lying around a museum isn't as interesting as one who chases people.

Mummies have starred in horror movies for over 60

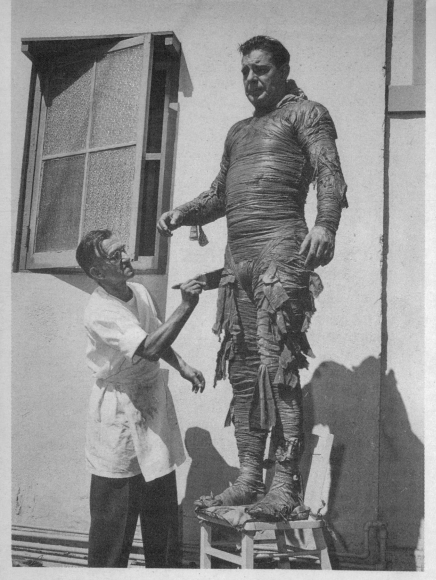

There have often been stories of people being mummified alive, and here is a photo that proves it! The actor getting wrapped up in his work is Lon Chaney, Jr. (The Bettmann Archive)

years. The discovery of King Tut's tomb increased interest around the world in Egyptian tombs and mummies. That's about the same time that movies were becoming very popular, too, so it's not surprising that mummies soon showed up in the movies.

Since silent movies are so hard to find, we'll talk only about sound movies. All of these movies you should be able to find in your local video store or on TV. The first really important mummy movie was made in 1932 and was called *The Mummy.* It was a big success and spawned a lot of imitations.

The Mummy (Universal Studios, 1932)

The Mummy, starring Boris Karloff, is still one of the scariest movies ever made. Because it was filmed only a few years after the discovery of King Tut's tomb, it's more authentic than most mummy movies.

The mummy, named Imhotep, isn't very authentic, because mummies do not come back to life. But most of the names, ceremonies, costumes, and sets in the movie are realistic. Right at the beginning of the movie, we see the real Valley of the Kings, which is dry desert mountains. The tomb itself looks old and dusty, which is certainly the way a real tomb would look.

The names of several Egyptian gods are used correctly. For example, the characters talk about Anubis being the god of tombs and mummies. We also see a statue of the cat-headed goddess Bast. In the movie, Bast is called the goddess of evil sendings, or wishes, but she was really the goddess of prayers.

In a flashback to ancient Egypt, we witness a funeral procession led by priests dressed up as gods, and that

The greatest movie mummy of all time, Imhotep, played by Boris Karloff in *The Mummy*. His makeup required eight hours to apply.   (The Bettmann Archive)

is very authentic. There is even a scene where the characters talk about dipping a mummy in natron.

While the filmmakers did some good research, the story centers on something that doesn't exist—a scroll that brings the dead back to life. It's called the Scroll of Thoth, and it supposedly has the magic words that the goddess Isis used to bring her husband, Osiris, back to life. Except for the scroll, the story of Isis and Osiris is a famous Egyptian legend.

If you're standing near a mummy, you don't want to read the Scroll of Thoth out loud. One character does, and he's sorry for it. Boris Karloff looks very real as the undead mummy, Imhotep, and the scene where he comes back to life is a classic.

The next time Imhotep shows up, the bandages are gone and he looks almost human, but he walks very stiffly and his face is terribly wrinkled. He tells the British explorers where another tomb is hidden, the tomb of a long-dead princess.

We learn in flashbacks to the past that Imhotep was once a respected priest who was in love with the beautiful princess. She died, and Imhotep tried to bring her back to life with the Scroll of Thoth. This was against the law, and he was wrapped in bandages and buried alive. (By the way, there have been a few Egyptian mummies who were buried alive—but they never came back to life either.)

Now the princess has been reincarnated in a living woman. Reincarnation is the belief that the soul comes back to Earth in a new body. However, the Egyptians never believed in reincarnation, so this part of the movie is not very realistic.

At this point, *The Mummy* begins to resemble another Universal movie, *Dracula.* Like Dracula, Imhotep uses his evil powers to try to win the beautiful girl away from her boyfriend and her protectors. You can guess how it ends, but it's still fun to watch.

The Mummy's Hand (Universal Studios, 1940), The Mummy's Tomb (Universal Studios, 1942), The Mummy's Ghost (Universal Studios, 1944), The Mummy's Curse (Universal Studios, 1944)

Universal made so much money on the original *The Mummy* that the studio made four more mummy movies. They aren't as scary or authentic as the first one, but they're still a lot of fun.

These movies are different from the original in that the mummy, named Kharis, stays wrapped up in his bandages the whole time. In *The Mummy's Hand,* Kharis is played by a cowboy actor named Tom Tyler. In the other three movies, Kharis is played by Lon Chaney Jr., who is also famous for playing the Wolfman.

Unlike Imhotep, Kharis is not brought back to life by the Scroll of Thoth. He is resurrected by a drink of tanna leaves brewed for him by an evil priest. George Zucco plays the priest in the first movie, followed by Turhan Bey and John Carradine in the other movies. Turhan Bey was actually an Egyptian, which makes his portrayal interesting.

These priests are upset at the explorers who keep digging up Egyptian tombs, and they use the mummy to get revenge. Unlike Imhotep, who talks and acts like a living person, Kharis is just a monster who tries to kill people. The priests are the brains behind Kharis, and they keep him in line with the tanna leaves.

A drink of three tanna leaves keeps Kharis alive, and

a drink with nine tanna leaves gets him up and seeking revenge. Shuffling along with one bad leg, it's a wonder he ever catches anybody, but he does.

Universal did keep part of the story from the original *The Mummy* with Boris Karloff. Kharis, too, was in love with a princess in ancient Egypt, and was buried alive for trying to bring her back to life. He had his tongue cut out, which is why he can't talk. His beloved, Princess Ananka, has similarly been reincarnated in the body of a living woman.

Through four movies, Kharis and his evil masters try to capture the reincarnated princess and return her to her tomb, but Kharis will not be killed, as long as there are tanna leaves. In fact, he returned almost 20 years later in a British horror movie.

The Mummy (Hammer Films, 1958)

Although it was made in England by another studio, this movie is a combination of all the Universal mummy movies. It's filmed in color and is very pretty to look at, but it seems far less authentic. The ancient tomb, for example, is found in a jungle oasis and looks like someone's living room.

As in the original 1932 version, the mummy is brought back to life by reading a mysterious scroll. Also like the other Universal movies, the mummy is named Kharis, and his job is to do whatever an evil priest tells him to do. He still loves a long-dead princess who is reincarnated in a living woman.

The best part of this movie is the flashback to ancient Egypt. The research comes through, as we learn that it takes 70 days to process a mummy. We witness a realistic funeral procession led by a priest wearing the jackal mask of Anubis, god of tombs and mummies. They even do something that looks like the Opening of the Mouth ceremony.

Christopher Lee, as Kharis, is very convincing in the flashback scenes in Egypt, but he's not so convincing as a mummy who walks around the English countryside. King Tut's Curse is a much easier way to get revenge on people who explore Egyptian tombs.

Funny Mummies

Whenever movie comics like the Three Stooges or Abbott and Costello get inside an Egyptian tomb, you can be sure that a mummy will soon be chasing them. A mummy makes a good monster in a comedy, because he's scary but so slow that it's easy to outrun him.

Some of these comedies are more realistic than horror movies, because the mummies often turn out to be people in disguise. The bad guys usually disguise themselves as mummies to scare the good guys away from something valuable inside the tomb.

Mummies also turn up in TV cartoon shows, like *Scooby Doo, Johnny Quest, Ghostbusters,* and *Dennis the Menace.* In fact, any cartoon show that involves travel to distant places will usually get around to visiting Egypt and finding mummies. If you see a mummy on TV, you can be pretty sure he's going to get up and chase somebody.

There is also a series of Mexican movies starring the Aztec Mummy. Never mind that the Aztec Indians didn't mummify their dead, like the Incas did. They had pyramids, so movie makers gave them mummies, too.

The Aztec Mummy is in the Kharis mode—he doesn't speak but chases people who try to take things out of his tomb.

The Aztec Mummy movies are not supposed to be comedies, but they can be pretty funny. The Aztec Mummy can be found guarding tombs in movies with titles like *Curse of the Aztec Mummy* and *Wrestling Women Versus the Aztec Mummy*. Don't watch them unless you really like bad movies.

These days, mummies are almost always used for comedy—like the guy in the gorilla suit—but it wasn't always that way. If you want to see a scary mummy movie, rent the video of the Boris Karloff original, *The Mummy*.

Chapter 8

Modern Research on Ancient Mummies

Mummies tell us something that ruined buildings and priceless relics can't tell us: what the bodies of our distant ancestors were like. Did they have toothaches? Did they catch colds? How different were they from us?

Four thousand years ago, the Egyptians were the most civilized people on Earth. They cultivated and farmed and built buildings that would be too expensive to build today. While Europeans were living in caves, ancient Egyptians resided in houses, had doctors, and went to school. They lived lives that were very peaceful for those times.

They were more like modern people than any other ancient people. So we wonder if they suffered from the same diseases. How long did they live? What was their diet like? Is a modern human being more healthy—or less healthy—than an ancient Egyptian?

Luckily, the Egyptians preserved their dead so well that modern researchers can examine them as if they had just died. If the mummy is in good condition, it can be given a "physical" with the same kind of tests that are used on living people, like X-rays, blood tests, CAT scans, and other modern techniques.

Royal mummies are particularly interesting because the royal family was very inbred. Inbreeding means that many brothers, sisters, and cousins married each other to keep the bloodline "pure." This is common for the system of government called a monarchy.

In a monarchy, the country is ruled by kings and queens all descended from a royal family. Like most monarchies, the rulers of Egypt maintained power by marrying within the same family. The result is a pure strain that is easy to identify through blood tests.

Blood of the Pharaohs

Many Egyptian mummies have enough blood cells left to study their blood as we would a living person's. For example, King Tutankhamen's blood was Group A, subgroup 2, with antigens M and N present. That's a rare bloodline that was common among the Pharaohs of the New Kingdom. Blood tests are often used to make sure that supposedly royal mummies are really royal.

Too much inbreeding could result in geniuses, like the great builder Rameses II; or it could result in Pharaohs that were mentally deficient. Many theorize that King Tut was a less-than-able ruler, accounting for his early death by a blow to the head.

We know Tut died from a blow to the head, because

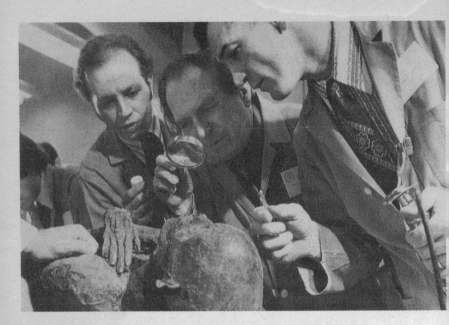

Scientists at the Smithsonian Institute study an Egyptian mummy. They use methods pioneered by coroners and pathologists to find out how ancient people died. (UPI/Bettmann)

his X-ray photographs were examined by coroners. If King Tut had died today instead of 3300 years ago, his death would surely be investigated as a homicide.

Not just blood, but hair and skin samples are taken from mummies. Remember how Egyptian embalmers removed the intestines and other organs and stored them separately? These organs have proven very valuable. Every part of a mummy, from its lungs to its fingernails, tells us something about the once-living person.

Tissue samples from hair, skin, and organs are studied under high-powered microscopes and tested in the laboratory using chemical analysis. These tests take us deep into the mummy's cell structure, to its DNA. DNA study has grown more important in recent years, because of diseases which change the cells in our bodies. Two such diseases are cancer and AIDS (Acquired Immune Deficiency Syndrome).

Like the common cold, we think AIDS is caused by a virus, but we don't know how to cure it. If we knew how old viruses were, or where they came from, we would have a better chance of fighting them. We think AIDS began in Africa, so researchers are studying blood, hair, and skin samples to see if Egyptian mummies show any signs of AIDS.

Research into mummies has only begun in this area, and it's hard to tell what information will be found from blood samples and genetic testing. Genetics can tell us if the Egyptians were likely to get a crippling disease like arthritis, but only X-ray tests can tell us which mummies actually suffered from arthritis.

Seeing Inside a Mummy

Most of what we know about mummies has been discovered through the use of X-ray tests. An X-ray test is a way to take a photograph of the inside of something. X-ray machines have been used to photograph shipwrecks at the bottom of the ocean, the dentist X-rays your teeth, and the doctor X-rays your broken arm. When you go on an airplane, your luggage is X-rayed to see if it contains any weapons.

For hundred of years, mummies were destroyed by unwrapping them in front of tourists and paying customers, but very little was learned from this carelessness. In 1895, the X-ray machine was invented, and researchers had a better way to look inside a mummy. By far, X-ray tests are the least harmful way to study a mummy.

Before museums had X-ray machines of their own, they often took their mummies to hospitals to be studied. Now there are portable X-ray machines that can be taken anywhere, and almost all mummies have been X-rayed. Here are some interesting facts about X-rayed mummies:

- X-ray test results often reveal surprises. As we mentioned before, many museums thought they had child mummies—only to learn through X-ray tests that they were really baboons. The strangest discovery is that some mummies contain parts of more than one person.

  Several female mummies contain the remains of a baby. It was apparently the custom to wrap a baby with its mother when both died in childbirth. But in one case, two babies and a ten-year-old child were wrapped up with a male mummy. In one mummy, there were two skulls! We'll never know why things like this happened, except that maybe the embalmers got lazy.

- X-ray tests are often used to identify mummies and determine family relationships. Many royal mummies were found in mass graves, having been moved there after their large tombs were plundered. X-ray test results of facial features—such as cheekbones, noses, and jaw structure—have often proven whether mummies were from the royal family or not.

80

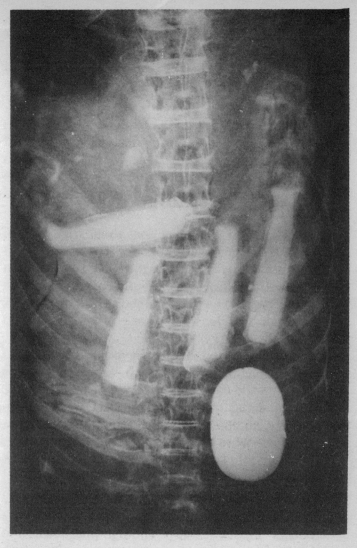

This X-ray photograph of the unwrapped mummy of Queen Notmet shows a large oval scarab and four small statues that were buried with her for protection. Many mummies were destroyed when tomb robbers tried to look for such riches. (UPI/Bettmann)

- X-ray tests tell us that Egyptians had many of the same health problems we have, including hardening of the arteries, polio, tuberculosis, arthritis, rheumatism, and gallstones.

- X-ray tests of the mummy's teeth, bones, and arteries give doctors a good idea how old the person was when he died, but they don't always reveal if the mummy is male or female. Many museums do not know the sex of the mummies they have on display, even if they know how old they were and how they died.

- X-ray tests tell us a great deal about what kind of food the Egyptians ate. Just like us, they had cavities and gum disease, so they must have eaten sweets. However, many Egyptians had bad teeth from eating food with too much sand in it, and this puzzled researchers for a long time. Why would people eat sand?

    They discovered that the Egyptians used sand to help them mill their grains. Milling grain means removing the dry outer covering of the grain, the husk, and then grinding the grain into flour. Apparently, adding sand helped the milling go faster, but it also wore down the Egyptians' teeth. Older Egyptians often didn't have any molars, or back teeth, left at all.

- X-ray photographs have revealed sacred amulets and jewelry inside the wrappings that the grave robbers missed. X-ray photographs have also shown that some mummies were repaired with metal clamps and wires, then rewrapped. This probably happened after they were disturbed by grave robbers.

- X-ray photographs also reveal, as in King Tut's case, whether or not the person died from violence. Some Egyptians died of head wounds and accidents, but the majority of them died of natural illnesses. Mummy X-ray photographs have confirmed that the ancient Egyptians were basically a peaceful people.

How Did They Die?

Most Egyptians lived to be only 35 to 40 years old. That is about 30 fewer years than we can expect to live today. Some Pharaohs and priests did live to be very old, but we can assume they had better medical care than the average Egyptian.

By the age of 40, an Egyptian was often suffering from arthritis, rheumatism, hardening of the arteries, or other illnesses that go along with old age, but that's not what killed most of them. They seldom died of cancer and heart disease, which are the major killers of our time. The Egyptians were probably healthier than we are, except for one thing—parasites.

Almost all Egyptian mummies show evidence of having been infected with parasites. The water of the Nile River brought life to the Egyptians, but it also brought death. Hundreds of different kinds of parasites lived in the river and entered the Egyptians' bodies when they drank or bathed, causing terrible sores and rashes and making their victims sick and weak. Eventually, the parasites laid eggs, multiplied, and grew—until they killed their host.

The Egyptians had many useful medicines, and their doctors performed operations, but they didn't have the antibiotics necessary to kill parasites. They could have

83

prevented much of their misery by boiling their water before they drank it. But the eggs of parasites are microscopic, and the Egyptians probably didn't know where their ailments came from.

The mighty Egyptians, master builders and embalmers, never learned how to defeat the tiny animals which killed so many of them.

Chapter 9

Cryonics—

Mummies of the Future?

Ancient people mummified bodies to honor the dead and provide a home for the soul. They believed strongly in an afterlife when the earthly life was over. A preserved body was a way in which the dead person's spirit could live both here and in the afterlife. Only in horror movies did a mummy ever come back to life.

The proof that ancient mummies were not supposed to come back to life is that most of their important organs were removed. Their skin was dried with chemicals, sunlight, and desert air. They were supposed to *look* lifelike, but they were not supposed to live again.

In today's society and religion, a dead body is not very important. Morticians make the body of a loved one look nice for the funeral, but there's no attempt to preserve it forever. We bury the body in the ground or burn it, which is called cremation. In our modern thinking, death is the end of the body. Even people who believe strongly in God and heaven don't think the body is necessary for the afterlife.

There are, however, some people who think death is *not* the end of the body. They think what we call "death" may be reversible. They want to preserve bodies through low-temperature freezing in order to revive them in the future. This process is called cryonic suspension, or cryonics.

What Is Death?

We used to think we knew what death was. Fifty years ago, when a heart stopped beating, that was death. Now, though, we can start a heart beating again and keep it beating for days or even years. We have artificial respirators that keep the lungs breathing. We have kidney dialysis machines, artificial hearts, and other machines that take the place of organs in our bodies, but the one organ we have never learned to replace is the brain. Therefore, when the brain stops functioning—called brain death—it is usually time to call the funeral home.

People who believe in cryonics think this is all wrong. There are constantly new discoveries in medicine, they say, and we have no idea what wonders there will be in a hundred years. Every day we learn more about the tiniest parts of our bodies: cells, molecules, DNA. We can't repair a brain cell today, but maybe we'll be able to repair it in the future.

Therefore, the cryonicists say, bodies should be frozen immediately after death. In some cases, they should be frozen *before* death, before the disease destroys large parts of the body. These people believe that diseases that

This is the inside of a chamber that is used for
cryonics—the freezing of human bodies. Using liquid
nitrogen, the unit freezes bodies at 195 degrees below
zero, Celsius. (UPI/Bettmann)

kill people today will be curable tomorrow. Then the bodies can be thawed out and revived to live again.

As you might guess, there is a lot of controversy about this idea. The majority of doctors say it's impossible. Even the cryonicists admit it is impossible—today. They are relying upon the future to make it possible.

The freezing part is no problem. The technology exists to freeze people very rapidly at very low temperatures (minus 320 degrees Fahrenheit, or minus 196 degrees Celsius). Thanks to cryobiologists, scientists who study the effects of freezing on animal life, we know a great deal about this process.

In fact, thousands of people have already had their bodies frozen after death. There are several organizations both here and in Europe that can make all the arrangements and perform the service. They claim to have the facilities to keep a body in cryonic suspension until it can be revived. It's expensive to have a whole body frozen, and most people pay for it with a life insurance policy.

Some people just have their heads frozen. Freezing a head is really just a simple way to freeze the brain so that it can be transplanted into another body in the future. Brains from mice and rabbits have been shown to still function after freezing, but no one can say for certain how human bodies and brains will be revived.

Revival

To understand how cryonics is supposed to work, think of a human body as a machine, like a car. When a car is parked and the engine is turned off, we could say it's "dead." Nothing but the battery is really alive

88

anymore. If the car is left long enough without running, even the battery will die. The structure of the car—the engine, radiator, tubes, pipes, spark plugs—is still all there. When you start the car again, the fuel pump will send gasoline to the engine, the pistons will pump, and the car will come back to life. People who believe in cryonics think the same thing can happen to a human body.

The problem is that our bodies are not made out of steel and rubber, but of organic material. As soon as blood and nourishment stops flowing through our bodies, the cells begin to deteriorate. They can't be brought back to life, and that is where the freezing comes in. Freezing the body immediately after death supposedly halts deterioration and keeps the structure of the cells intact.

Since human beings are mostly water, freezing will normally turn a body into ice, like a giant Popsicle. To prevent this, cryonicists pump a liquid called glycerol into the body before freezing it. (Glycerol is the same substance that is used to make antifreeze for a car radiator.) When the body is frozen with glycerol, there is less damage to the cells and blood vessels.

If the basic structure of the cells is intact, cryonicists believe, the body can be repaired and revived. The technology to do this doesn't exist today, but some scientists think we'll have microscopic repair machines in the future. These nanomachines will enter the bloodstream, remove ice, and repair cells. They will even cure the disease which killed the person, but it would probably take many months to revive a body.

Today, the idea of nanomachines and molecular repair is pure theory, but so at one time were airplanes, heart transplants, television, and space shuttles.

Mummies of the Future

We can't say today whether any frozen bodies will ever be revived, but we can say for certain that cryonics preserves a body better than natron, caves, bogs, or any other process. Freezing preserves everything: organs, nerves, blood vessels, skin, bones, and muscle.

You might remember from an earlier chapter that one of the best-preserved accidental mummies was an Eskimo woman frozen in ice. Her skin was still soft and pliable. A baby mammoth was still in good shape after 27,000 years under the ice. After cave mummies have turned to dust, frozen mummies will still be as fresh as the day they fell into the ice.

Maybe we shouldn't be so fast to condemn cryonics. Even if the cryonicists never manage to revive a single frozen body, they are creating mummies that scientists can study thousands of years from now. Future scientists will be just as anxious to learn about us as we are to learn about ancient Egyptians and Bog People.

Today we preserve buildings, paintings, plays, books, forests, and even movies because we want to leave them for future generations. Cryonics is carrying on a tradition that started thousands of years ago—preserving the human body for eternity.